Elements

CALCIUM AND MAGNESIUM

Ca

Mg

Grolier Educational

SHERMAN TURNPIKE, DANBURY, CONNECTICUT 06816

How to use this book

j546
v.3
(3)

This book has been carefully developed to help you understand the chemistry of the elements. In it you will find a systematic and comprehensive coverage of the basic qualities of each element. Each two-page entry contains information at various levels of technical content and language, along with definitions of useful technical terms, as shown in the thumbnail diagram to the right. There is a comprehensive glossary of technical terms at the back of the book, along with an extensive index, key facts, an explanation of the periodic table, and a description of how to interpret chemical equations.

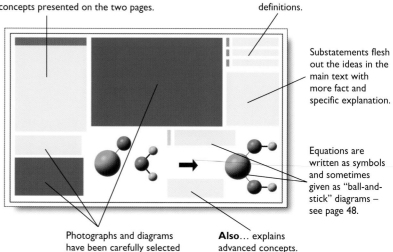

The main text follows the sequence of information in the book and summarizes the concepts presented on the two pages.

Technical definitions.

Substatements flesh out the ideas in the main text with more fact and specific explanation.

Equations are written as symbols and sometimes given as "ball-and-stick" diagrams – see page 48.

Photographs and diagrams have been carefully selected and annotated for clarity.

Also... explains advanced concepts.

Author
Brian Knapp, BSc, PhD
Project consultant
Keith B. Walshaw, MA, BSc, DPhil
        (Head of Chemistry, Leighton Park School)
Industrial consultant
Jack Brettle, BSc, PhD (Chief Research Scientist, Pilkington plc)
Art Director
Duncan McCrae, BSc
Editor
Elizabeth Walker, BA
Special photography
Ian Gledhill
Illustrations
David Woodroffe
Electronic page makeup
Julie James Graphic Design
Designed and produced by
EARTHSCAPE EDITIONS
Print consultants
Landmark Production Consultants Ltd
Reproduced by
Leo Reprographics
Printed in Hong Kong by
Wing King Tong Company Ltd

**First published in the United States in 1996 by
Grolier Educational, Sherman Turnpike,
Danbury, CT 06816**

**First reprint 1997, second reprint 1997, and third reprint
2000. New and revised edition 2002**

Copyright © 1996 & 2002
Atlantic Europe Publishing Company Limited

Cataloging information may be obtained directly from Grolier Educational.

Volumes 1-18 Set ISBN: 0–7172–5674–X
Volume 3 ISBN: 0–7172–7575–2
Library of Congress Number: 95–082222
Dewey: 546—dc21

Acknowledgments
The publishers would like to thank the following for their kind help and advice: *Jonathan Frankel* of J.M. Frankel and Associates, *Ian* and *Catherine Gledhill* of Shutters, *John Chrobnick*, *Steve Rockell* of Goodrock Properties Services Ltd, *Pippa Trounce* and *Mike L. Willoughby*.

Picture credits
All photographs by **Earthscape Editions**.
Front cover: A piece of fossil-rich oolitic limestone. Limestone is mostly white calcium carbonate but in this case is reddish due to iron staining and some contamination by mud.
Title page: Desert roses, a compound of calcium called calcium sulfate.

*This product is manufactured from sustainable
managed forests. For every tree cut down at
least one more is planted.*

The demonstrations described or illustrated in this book are not for replication. The Publisher cannot accept any responsibility for any accidents or injuries that may result from conducting the experiments described or illustrated in this book.

Contents

Introduction

An element is a substance that cannot be broken down into a simpler substance by any known means. Each of the 92 naturally occurring elements is a fundamental substance from which everything in the Universe is made. This book is about calcium and magnesium and is one of a series on the elements.

Calcium

Probably everyone has watched a teacher use a stick of "chalk" to mark a blackboard. Blackboard chalk is a calcium-rich material. It is a compound containing the element calcium, (symbol Ca) bonded together with one other element or more. Calcium on its own is actually a soft, silvery-colored metal. However, calcium only occurs in nature as part of compounds.

The most common calcium compound is a material called calcium carbonate. Most people know calcium carbonate as rock, such as chalk, limestone and marble. They may have admired coral reefs without realizing that both the coral rock and the tiny green plants that live with the coral, known as algae, have calcium in them. Calcium even contributes to the pearls that are used to make rings and necklaces.

When gardeners use crushed limestone, crushed bone meal, or pulverized shell as a soil-improver in their gardens, few may realize that the bones of animals as well as the shells of snails, mussels and myriad other creatures contain calcium.

The bones of people also have calcium compounds in them. In fact, about one-fiftieth of the human body is made from calcium. Some uses you may be able to guess, such as the formation of bones and teeth, but others are quite invisible to us, such as making our muscles move!

But the element calcium is not just in natural things. For example, it is also in the walls of the house around you. Its compounds make up the plaster used in walls, the cement that holds bricks firmly together and concrete that makes the base for the house.

Magnesium

In many ways magnesium (symbol Mg) is very similar to calcium. Magnesium is one of the most important metals in the body, making up no less than one-fortieth of each and every one of us. It is also a very important element in the makeup of all green plants.

Like calcium, magnesium is never naturally found alone but always as a compound combined with other elements. For example, it makes up the hard limestone-looking rocks of magnesium carbonate called dolomite. Magnesium carbonate is used as a filler in paper and as an antacid. And because magnesium burns with an intense white light, it is also useful as a signal flare.

This book will introduce you to some of the wide range of properties of calcium, magnesium and some of the compounds they form. It is a starting point for your exciting exploration into the world of chemistry.

▲ Calcium metal burns with a brick-red colored flame. The flame test is an important way to look for the presence of calcium.

Calcium

Calcium is a soft silvery-colored metal that reacts with other elements to form compounds. In fact, it reacts so easily that it is never found on its own in nature.

If you see calcium metal in a laboratory, it will often be in the form of small pieces called pellets. This is to make it easy to use in experiments like the one shown on these pages. With pellets it is possible to demonstrate how calcium reacts with one of the most common compounds of all – water.

❷▼ A small pellet of calcium is placed in a beaker of water. To start with it sinks, showing that it is heavier than water.

A test tube filled with water is placed over the pellet. Notice that bubbles of hydrogen gas are already rising through the water. This is a result of the reaction of calcium with water.

❶▼ Calcium rapidly reacts with oxygen in the air to form a protective (dull) coating that tends to prevent any further reaction. It only looks silvery when freshly cut.

These calcium pellets look dark because of a surface coating of calcium oxide.

A calcium pellet is placed in a beaker of water and under a test tube.

❸▼ The calcium pellet rises up the test tube, buoyed by bubbles of hydrogen gas.

The solution in the test tube quickly becomes saturated with calcium hydroxide from the reaction. Calcium hydroxide now forms tiny particles (precipitate), making the water appear cloudy.

The hydrogen gas released by the vigorous reaction between the calcium pellet and the water soon fills the test tube.

compound: a chemical consisting of two or more elements chemically bonded together.

precipitate: tiny solid particles formed as a result of a chemical reaction between two liquids or gases.

reaction: the recombination of two substances using parts of each substance to produce new substances.

saturated: a state in which a liquid can hold no more of a substance. If any more of the substance is added, it will not dissolve.

The cloudiness in the water is caused by particles of calcium hydroxide.

❹▲ On reaching the surface the bubbles burst and the calcium pellet again sinks down into the beaker. Each time the reaction becomes more violent and the bubbles become bigger. Big bubbles like this can form when the oxide coating has been removed, allowing the metal to react more rapidly. The reaction also gives out heat. The precipitate of calcium hydroxide is granular, remaining suspended in the water for some time and making it cloudy.

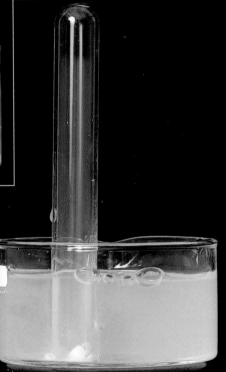

❺▲ The calcium bobs up and down in the water for a while and then stays on the surface because the calcium pellet gets so small it is more and more easily lifted to the surface by bubbles.

The tube fills with hydrogen and all the water is pushed out of the tube. This stops the reaction.

EQUATION: Calcium in water

Calcium + water ⇨ hydrogen gas + calcium hydroxide

$$Ca(s) \quad + \quad 2H_2O(l) \quad ⇨ \quad H_2(g) \quad + \quad Ca(OH)_2(aq)$$

(calcium hydroxide solution is also known as limewater)

Crystals containing calcium

The most common compound of calcium is limestone, calcium carbonate. This is often a dull gray rock, but occasionally, in small cavities in the rocks, it makes crystals, and the true brilliance of the mineral shows through. The crystalline form of calcium carbonate is called calcite.

Calcite can be found all over the world. It often occurs along with rare metals. In fact, because it is so common and has such a sparkling white color, it is very easy to spot. It has led prospectors to find such metals as gold and tin, silver and copper.

Forms of calcite

There is a pure, completely transparent version of calcite. It is known as Iceland Spar because it is sometimes found in cavities in solidified lava, of which Iceland is made. When you look into a piece of Iceland Spar, you actually see double because it has the wonderful property of showing two images of anything you see through it.

More often, calcite forms sparkling white crystals, which are sometimes found on the surface near hot springs. Geologists call this material travertine (see pages 16 and 17). It was the most widely used building stone of ancient Rome.

Other calcium-rich crystals

Calcium compounds can also make crystals known as "Blue John," a corruption of the French words *bleu* and *jaune* for blue and yellow. Geologists call it fluorspar (calcium fluoride) and it makes beautiful green, blue and yellow cubic crystals.

▼ These are desert roses, a compound of calcium called calcium sulfate (also called gypsum). The crystals of this mineral look a bit like rose petals, hence its name. It has a different look from the more blocklike rhombic crystals of calcite.

◄ This fossil ammonite has been cut in half so that you can see how its original form has been replaced by calcite. The calcite appears as the gray in-filling to the shell segments. In a few cases you can see how the calcite has formed in small cavities, giving delicate crystals.

lava: the material that flows from a volcano.

mineral: a solid substance made of just one element or chemical compound. Calcite is a mineral because it consists only of calcium carbonate; halite is a mineral because it contains only sodium chloride; quartz is a mineral because it consists of only silicon dioxide.

prospector: a person who is exploring for geologically rich deposits of metals and gemstones.

► This rhombohedral-shaped crystal is typical of calcite. The faces are parallelograms.

► Crystals of calcite growing in a small cavity in a limestone rock. Notice the limestone fossils. There are more examples of fossils cast in limestone on the next page.

Limestone

Limestone is the common name for rocks that are made up mainly of calcium carbonate. Limestones vary greatly and have many origins.

The origins of limestone

Most limestone rocks share an origin in ancient warm, shallow seas. Some were formed as vast coral reefs. Others were formed from the cemented remains of tiny sea creatures and made into soft chalk. The warm waters also caused calcium to precipitate out from sea waters rather like the scale in a kettle. This scale took the form of millions of tiny balls of limestone. This type of limestone is called oolitic limestone after the Greek word *oon*, meaning egg-shaped.

Water-bearing rocks

Most limestones have cracks and gaps that make them porous. Oil and water can then accumulate in these gaps. This is what makes limestone good oil-bearing and water-bearing rock.

The color of limestone

Limestone is rarely white because of the impurities in it. It is most commonly light gray, a result of a mixture of calcite and mud. Oolitic limestone is often honey-colored because it contains some iron. Limestones can contain so much iron that they are worth mining as iron ore.

▲ This is a quarry in Portland. Limestone is one of the world's most famous building stones.

coral reef: a region of the seabed where corals grow in massive banks.

ore: a rock containing enough of a useful substance to make mining it worthwhile.

porous: containing many small holes or cracks. Quite often the pores are connected together, and liquids, such as water or oil, can move through them.

▼ Bands of limestone weather differently when exposed to the air, sometimes creating spectacular landscapes called karst scenery.

▲ A piece of fossil-rich limestone. The body of the limestone is made up of tiny limestone balls (it is oolitic limestone). The reddish coloring is due to iron staining.

◀ This limestone is made up of corals that became engulfed in a gray, lime-containing mud.

Dissolving limestone

Although calcium carbonate (limestone) will not dissolve in pure water, it will react easily with an acid. The reaction happens naturally as acidic rainwater seeps through soils and reaches limestone rocks.

Carbon dioxide, a gas found naturally in the atmosphere, dissolves in raindrops and produces carbonic acid. Its effect on limestone is slow but unceasing. More carbon dioxide is produced in the tiny passageways of soil. This dissolves in the water, seeps down to rocks and causes underground limestone to react and dissolve faster than surface rock.

This slow natural solution of the rock is called weathering. Sometimes the surface soil is stripped off a limestone rock and you can see the way the joints have been widened by chemical weathering (see next page). In some cases the joints are widened enough to produces holes big enough to swallow entire rivers.

▼ Sink holes

Sink holes are depressions in the surface of limestone that have been produced by extreme solution of the limestone blocks.

As the blocks dissolve away, they are no longer able to support each other, and they collapse.

Sink holes may be the entrances to entire cave systems, and rivers may disappear into them. This example is in the Tarn Valley in southern France.

EQUATION: Dissolving limestone

Water + carbon dioxide ⇨ carbonic acid

$$H_2O(l) \quad + \quad CO_2(g) \quad ⇨ \quad H_2CO_3(aq)$$

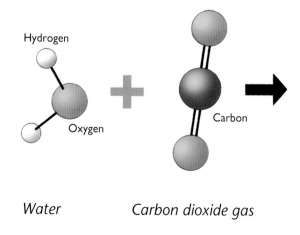

Hydrogen

Oxygen

Carbon

Water

Carbon dioxide gas

dissolve: to break down a substance in a solution without reacting.

solution: a mixture of a liquid and at least one other substance.

weathering: the slow natural processes that break down rocks and reduce them to small fragments either by mechanical or chemical means.

The faster effects of pollution

Weathering is an example of a general chemical process called corrosion. But in urban areas, and those suffering from acid rain, carbon dioxide is not the only gas in the rainwater. Sulfur dioxide and several oxides of nitrogen are also present. These pollutants are produced by burning fossil fuels. They produce a more concentrated acid, and the weathering effect is much more rapid.

Corrosion produced by acid rain has destroyed many of the limestone sculptures on famous buildings such as ancient cathedrals.

◀ This limestone sculpture on Reims cathedral in France is corroding because of pollution gases in the rainwater.

EQUATION: Dissolving limestone

Carbonic acid + calcium carbonate ⇨ calcium bicarbonate

$$H_2CO_3(aq) \quad + \quad CaCO_3(s) \quad ⇨ \quad Ca(HCO_3)_2(aq)$$

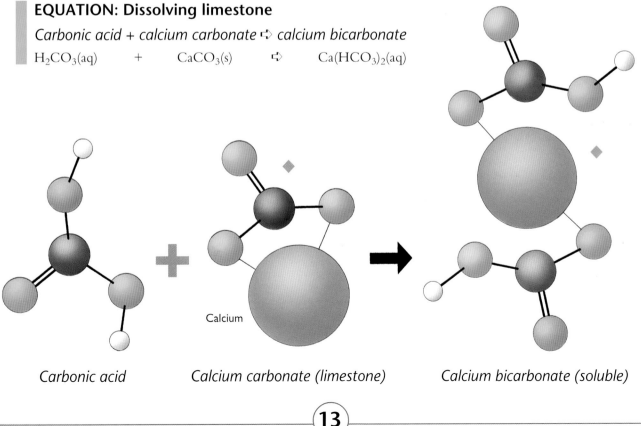

Calcium

Carbonic acid   *Calcium carbonate (limestone)*   *Calcium bicarbonate (soluble)*

Caves and caverns

Calcium-containing materials are precipitated in many forms in caves and passages underground. They may form sheets of stone that mask the cave walls, rising columns called stalagmites, or descending columns called stalactites. However, each is made as water laden with calcium carbonate seeps into the caves.

How water becomes rock

The calcium in hard water cannot be seen as it percolates out of tiny cracks in the walls and roofs of the cave. The water looks entirely clear. This is because the calcium is contained as calcium bicarbonate, a transparent solution.

As the water enters the cave, some of the dissolved carbon dioxide escapes, and as a result calcium carbonate is precipitated as tiny crystals of calcite, known as travertine. Over time these build into the fantastic forms inside some caves.

Cave formations

The shape that grows depends on the way the water drips from the roof and walls. If it drains over the walls, then curtain stalactites or flowstone curtains will form. But if it drips vertically, then stalactites will form on the roof of the cave, and stalagmites will form directly below, at the point where the water drips onto the floor.

Stalactites are not solid but rather consist of conical tubes. The water flows down the center of each tube and deposits more crystals on the outside edges of the drip. Stalagmites are thicker and more rounded in shape than stalactites and are solid rather than hollow.

The chemical precipitation takes place very slowly. In fact, it is uncommon for a stalactite to grow at rate greater than 2 mm a year. Stalactites that are many meters long are therefore very old.

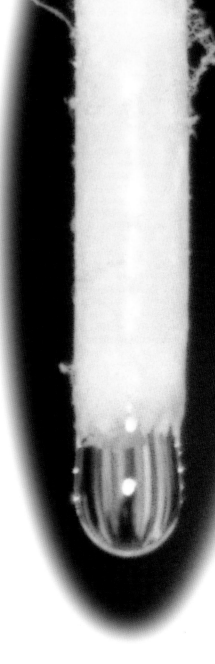

◀ Stalagmites, Carlsbad Caverns, New Mexico.

▼ Small wind-distorted stalactites, Caverns of Sonora, Texas.

mineral-laden: a solution close to saturation.

percolate: to move slowly through the pores of a rock.

◀ When water drips out of cracks in a cave, some of the carbon dioxide gas escapes from the water and the calcium bicarbonate changes to calcium carbonate (insoluble limestone). This is precipitated as a tiny addition to the cave. This picture shows a dripping limestone stalactite, Jenolan Caves, Australia.

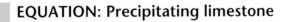

EQUATION: Precipitating limestone

Calcium bicarbonate ⇨ carbon dioxide + water + calcium carbonate

$$Ca(HCO_3)_2(aq) \quad ⇨ \quad CO_2(g) \quad + \quad H_2O(l) \quad + \quad CaCO_3(s)$$

solution   precipitate

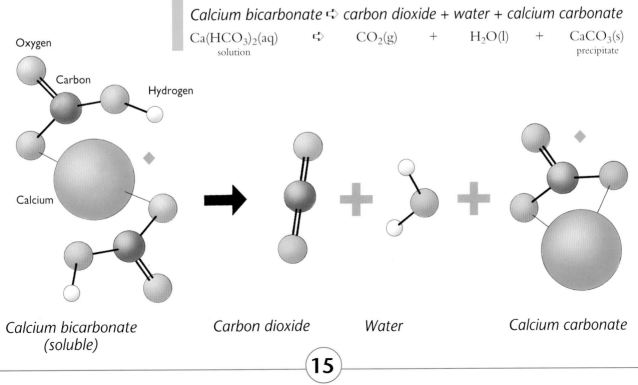

Oxygen

Carbon

Hydrogen

Calcium

Calcium bicarbonate (soluble)

Carbon dioxide

Water

Calcium carbonate

Calcium carbonate

◀ Calcium sinter

Because calcium bicarbonate is far less stable in hot water than in cold, just like the limescale on a kettle, calcium carbonate (travertine) is often precipitated around many hot springs.

The water in hot springs may have begun as pure rainwater; but by the time it has circulated through underground passages, it has dissolved much of the rock through which it is passing and thus has picked up considerable amounts of calcium compounds in solution. As this hot water reaches the ground, it cools and the calcium carbonate is precipitated as sheets of white calcite crystals that sparkle in the sunshine.

Waterfalls that sparkle

In the most spectacular locations, such as Pammukale in Turkey and Mammoth Hot Springs in Wyoming (shown here), calcite makes beautiful stepped pools of travertine.

The streaks of other colors in the travertine are formed by other minerals or mud. The pools are enclosed by rimstone dams. These are formed as the water flows over the rim where it is more likely to evaporate. This leads to a buildup of carbonate precipitate, which increases the height of the dam wall.

Calcium sinter

Geysers are dramatic forms of hot springs, sending out gushes of hot, mineral-rich water, sometimes containing calcite, on other occasions, silica-rich minerals. As the wind catches the spray of these natural fountains, it may wash over debris and coat it with hardened calcite, forming a sinter. In this way pieces of twig or other small objects can be fossilized.

calcite: the crystalline form of calcium carbonate.

precipitate: tiny solid particles formed as a result of a chemical reaction between two liquids or gases.

stable: able to exist without changing into another substance.

▼ Mammoth Hot Springs, Yellowstone National Park, Wyoming.

17

Building stone

The most common form of building stone that uses calcium-rich material is made of calcium carbonate, usually in the form of limestone. Many limestones are easy to cut up into blocks and so make good building stones. Calcium carbonate is also found as marble.

Limestone

Limestone is used the world over by architects to make buildings. It is reasonably hard, quite attractive, and yet can be easily sculpted and cut in any direction. Limestone comes from quarries where thick bands of rock are found.

Sometimes limestones are chosen for the fossils they contain. When cut and polished, the fossils make interesting decorations.

Limestone will react with rainwater and weather over a period of time. This can readily be seen in many old buildings.

Marble

Marble is limestone that has been naturally altered by millions of years in the depths of ancient mountains. The impurities show up as the mottling and streaks: red for iron, blue for graphite (a form of carbon) and so on. The streaks were formed when the marble became so hot that the impurities began to melt and run through the limestone.

Marble is much harder than limestone and more difficult to work with. It is used as the facing for many buildings and for some of the world's finest sculptures. Buildings containing huge amounts of marble include the White House in Washington DC and the Taj Mahal in India.

▲ The Capitol Building, Washington, DC, uses marble siding to provide a striking appearance.

▲ The Taj Mahal, India, the world's most famous marble-clad building.

▼ A piece of marble.

facing: sheets of stone cut to form the decorative outer surface of a building. It is a form of cladding. On modern buildings it is also sometimes called siding.

weather: a term used by Earth scientists and derived from "weathering." It means to react with water and gases of the environment.

▲ Vezelay Abbey, France. Notice how rainwater containing carbon dioxide has begun to dissolve the limestone. The effect is most noticeable on the corners of each block, giving each of the blocks a more rounded appearance.

▶ The Radcliffe Camera, Oxford University, England, a building made from a cream-colored limestone.

19

Calcium oxide

Calcium oxide, also known as quicklime, is a major constituent of every bag of cement you buy.

If limestone (calcium carbonate) is heated in a kiln, it will decompose to produce carbon dioxide gas and create a white solid of calcium oxide. A laboratory demonstration of the effect is shown here.

❶▼ The apparatus below shows how a small block of calcium carbonate (limestone) can be made into calcium oxide in the laboratory. It consists of an iron cylinder (the kiln) with a tray on which the limestone rests.

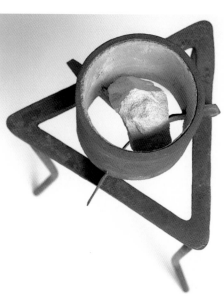

❷▶ A cover is put over the kiln and the limestone heated using a Bunsen burner. The limestone decomposes to form a white solid, called calcium oxide or quicklime, and gives off carbon dioxide gas. In the picture you can see the limestone glowing a yellow–red color.

base: a compound that may be soapy to the touch and that can react with an acid in water to form a salt and water.

decompose: to break down a substance (for example, by heat or with the aid of a catalyst) into simpler components. In such a chemical reaction only one substance is involved.

kiln: a structure designed for baking minerals. Lime, brick and pottery kilns are all common.

Rotary kiln (red tube)

◄▲ In a cement plant one of the larger pieces of equipment is an iron tube, slightly tilted down at one end and slowly rotating. Inside, limestone is roasted using a gas flame. This equipment, known as a rotating kiln, is the industrial equivalent of the process shown opposite.

EQUATION: Calcium carbonate decomposes

Calcium carbonate ⇨ calcium oxide + carbon dioxide

$$CaCO_3(s) \quad ⇨ \quad CaO(s) \quad + \quad CO_2(g)$$

❸◄ This picture shows what calcium oxide looks like after it has been cooled and then removed from the kiln.

Also...

Calcium oxide is a strong base and can be used to neutralize acids. Its violent reaction with water makes it unsuitable to be used directly as a soil conditioner (see calcium hydroxide, page 24). However, in dry form it can be used in the manufacture of cement, mortar and concrete.

Calcium carbonate breaks down when heated to form calcium oxide and releases carbon dioxide gas.

The technical word for this kind of breakdown is "thermal decomposition." However, this reaction is reversible. If carbon dioxide gas flows over calcium oxide, it will re-form calcium carbonate (although it will never again look like the original rock).

Using calcium oxide

Lime is a grayish white powder made by heating limestone. Lime (also called quicklime, see page 20) is one of the most important chemicals known, being sixth after salt, coal, sulfur, air, and water in the amounts used in our world. It is used as a foundation for making many other chemicals.

Mortar

Lime has been used since early times as a simple form of cement known as a mortar. When lime reacts with water, it gives off heat and changes to a new material that is an adhesive (glue). As the water evaporates, the mortar hardens.

Over time carbon dioxide gas, a natural part of the atmosphere, reacts with the mortar, turning it back into the calcium carbonate from which it was originally made. It then falls away as a white powder.

Glass

Lime is used in the making of glass, where it adds hardness and makes the glass insoluble.

Burials and compost heaps

Lime is also a nasty substance to deal with in its pure form. It is caustic, can burn the skin and cause trouble if the powder is breathed in. Lime was traditionally used in burials to hasten the decomposition of bodies.

▲ In the interests of economy these Balinese Geruda images have been cast in concrete although they used to be carved from basalt.

◄ **Whitewash paint**
This old house is made of natural boulders. It has been painted with whitewash, a mixture of lime and water.

Because lime picks up carbon dioxide from the air, it eventually turns back into chalk. Thus, the surface of whitewashed walls is often dusty.

Whitewash is cheap, but it has to be reapplied more often than modern paints.

▼ Most apartments are now made almost entirely with concrete. These are in Hong Kong.

Cement: calcium "glue"

One of the main uses of calcium compounds is in the manufacture of cement. Like mortar, cement is an adhesive (glue) used to bond bricks together or to bind stones and gravel to make concrete. Most cement is called Portland cement, a general kind of cement mix named after the English limestone (called Portland Stone) that was used in the cement patented by Joseph Aspdin in 1824.

Making cement

Cement is made from a combination of a limestone or chalk and a clay. The raw materials are ground down and then mixed together. Once mixed they are roasted in a kiln that constantly rotates. The roasting temperature is very high, about the same as that used to melt glass (1350°C). The material is then cooled and crushed to make a fine gray powder.

Using cement

Cement powder is mixed with water to make cement, a gray pasty substance. The chemical reaction that takes place happens very quickly; and if nothing were done to slow down the process, the cement would get hard in a few minutes and so be very difficult to use. The key to slowing down the reaction is to add gypsum (calcium sulfate).

Cement will last for many decades, but it is not as long-lasting as most other building materials. When exposed to the weather, it will eventually return to the calcium carbonate from which it was made.

Calcium hydroxide

Calcium hydroxide is a white solid. You may have seen cartons containing it in a garden shop under the name of "slaked lime" or "hydrated lime," where it is sold as a soil conditioner.

Calcium hydroxide can be formed by adding water to calcium oxide. The effect of this is shown on this page. It is a reaction that gives out considerable amounts of heat.

Another way of obtaining calcium hydroxide is shown on page 7, but calcium is too expensive to obtain as a metal for widespread industrial use.

❶▼ In the demonstration on this page, a block of calcium oxide (quicklime) is placed on a tray. Water is now poured onto one side of the block. This is so that changes that happen to the side in contact with water can then be compared to the original state of the calcium oxide, in its dry form.

The reaction is spectacular. The water soaks into the calcium oxide and disappears. The part of the block of quicklime in contact with the water gets extremely hot, swells and gives off steam. (There is a picture of the original solid on page 21.)

EQUATION: The formation of calcium hydroxide

Calcium oxide + water ⇨ calcium hydroxide

$$CaO(s) \quad + \quad H_2O(l) \quad ⇨ \quad Ca(OH)_2(aq)$$

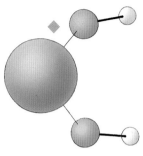

Oxygen

Hydrogen

Calcium

Calcium oxide   *Water*

Calcium hydroxide

base: a compound that may be soapy to the touch and that can react with an acid in water to form a salt and water.

ion: an atom, or group of atoms, that has gained or lost one or more electrons and so developed an electrical charge.

❷▼ The block of quicklime expands and begins to crack. Eventually it collapses to a "dry" powder, calcium hydroxide.

Also...

Calcium hydroxide is a strong base and can be used to neutralize acids. It can thus be spread onto an acid soil to neutralize it and provide better conditions for plant growth. Some of the calcium hydroxide breaks apart in water to yield a solution of positively charged calcium ions (Ca^{2+}) and negatively charged hydroxide ions (OH^-). In this state the calcium ions can cause soil particles to stick together (flocculate). Calcium ions can also be taken up in water present in soil and used by plants for growth.

Limewater

In the demonstration on pages 6 and 7, you will have noticed that, as the calcium pellet becomes smaller, the water becomes more cloudy. This is because the reaction with water produces a new solution, known as limewater – calcium hydroxide.

When limewater is saturated, calcium hydroxide is precipitated. A precipitate can be made to appear and disappear at will, as the following demonstration shows.

◀ Solution created by reacting a calcium pellet with water (see page 7) is passed down a glass rod through a filter paper in a funnel. A clear solution of calcium hydroxide passes out of the funnel and is collected in the beaker.

❶▶ As the calcium pellet reacts, it forms calcium hydroxide from the water. Calcium hydroxide is not very soluble in water. If the calcium pellet is large, the solution will contain as much calcium hydroxide as possible. This solution is known as a saturated solution. As more calcium reacts, it will not be possible for more calcium hydroxide to be kept in solution and so the surplus is made into tiny solid particles. This change from solution to solid is called precipitation. The suspension of these tiny particles in the liquid is what causes it to become cloudy. The particles eventually settle out on the bottom of the beaker, leaving the solution clear. They can be filtered from the solution leaving a clear liquid.

❷▶ Blowing a stream of bubbles into limewater using a straw produces a startling effect. When one breathes through the straw, the liquid appears milky.

Breath contains carbon dioxide gas. This reacts with the calcium hydroxide solution, producing calcium carbonate, which is much less soluble in water. The calcium carbonate is seen as tiny white particles and so the liquid becomes cloudy.

EQUATION: Limewater to calcium carbonate

Calcium hydroxide + carbon dioxide ⇨ calcium carbonate + water

$$Ca(OH)_2(aq) \quad + \quad CO_2(g) \quad \Rightarrow \quad Ca(CO)_3(s) \quad + \quad H_2O(l)$$

❸▼ If you keep blowing through the straw, the solution quickly goes clear again because the additional amount of carbon dioxide reacts with the calcium carbonate to produce soluble, and colorless, calcium bicarbonate, just like the rainwater and limestone described on page 13.

precipitate: tiny solid particles formed as a result of a chemical reaction between two liquids or gases.

solution: a mixture of a liquid and at least one other substance (e.g., saltwater). Mixtures can be separated by physical means, for example, by evaporation and cooling.

EQUATION: Calcium carbonate to calcium bicarbonate

Calcium carbonate + water + carbon dioxide ⇨ *calcium bicarbonate*

$$CaCO_3(s) \quad + \quad H_2O(l) \quad + \quad CO_2(g) \quad \Rightarrow \quad Ca(HCO_3)_2(aq)$$

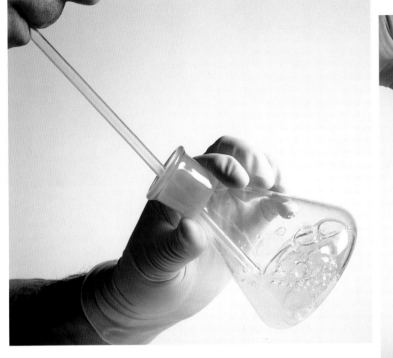

❹▶ Boiling the colorless solution will turn the solution cloudy again because calcium bicarbonate is not stable in hot water and the bicarbonate changes back to calcium carbonate, which is insoluble.

EQUATION: Change from calcium bicarbonate solution to calcium carbonate

Calcium bicarbonate solution ⇨ *calcium carbonate + carbon dioxide + water*

$$Ca(HCO_3)_2(aq) \quad \underset{\text{with heat}}{\Rightarrow} \quad CaCO_3(s) \quad + \quad CO_2(g) \quad + \quad H_2O(l)$$

Calcium in the soil

Calcium compounds are used in a soil to improve its condition and to balance any acidity. This means keeping the soil materials clumped together into crumb-sized pieces so that the soil drains well and air can get in. For this purpose calcium compounds are used as a form of "glue," holding the fine clay particles clumped into the size of sand grains.

Several compounds of calcium are used for this purpose. The fastest-acting compound is calcium hydroxide (slaked lime, often just called lime by gardeners), which readily breaks down in the soil. A more slow-acting compound is crushed limestone, calcium carbonate.

Lime is not always the best choice for a soil conditioner, however, because it will make a soil alkaline, and plants do not like too alkaline conditions any more than they like acid conditions. This is why it is now more common to apply finely crushed limestone. The limestone will simply remain in the soil until it is dissolved by acid water. In effect the crushed limestone is ready to neutralize the soil when needed but does not cause any damage when not required.

▶ This picture is an illustration of what happens in soil at a microscopic level. The small balls represent calcium ions that are attracted to pieces of clay by electrical charges (see "Also..."). There is always a balance between the calcium ions in the water and those on the soil surfaces. These calcium ions can also be sucked up by plants with soil water.

EQUATION: Neutralization in soil

Hydroxide ions + hydrogen ions ⇨ water

$$OH^-(aq) \quad + \quad H^+(aq) \quad ⇨ \quad H_2O(l)$$

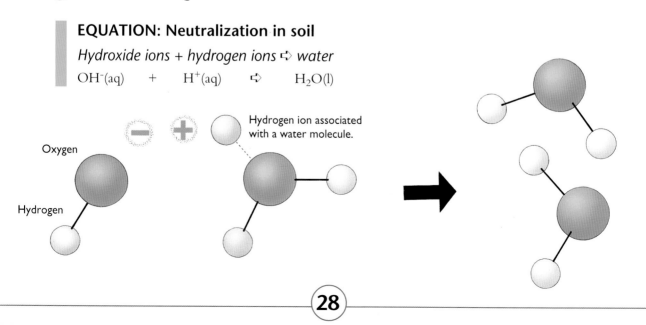

Oxygen

Hydrogen

Hydrogen ion associated with a water molecule.

acidity: a general term for the strength of an acid in a solution.

anion: a negatively charged atom or group of atoms.

cation: a positively charged atom or group of atoms.

ion: an atom, or group of atoms, that has gained or lost one or more electrons and so developed an electrical charge.

◀ Farmers sometimes apply calcium compounds to their fields to help the properties of the soil.

▼ This is a microscope picture of a soil. Notice how there are large gaps (light tone) between the soil particles (dark objects). These pores are where water is stored.

Root hair

Clay particles clumped, or flocculated, by calcium ions.

Calcium ions

Also...

Calcium hydroxide exists as two types of charged particles (known as ions): calcium ions (which are positively charged, or cations) and hydroxide ions (which are negatively charged, or anions). The hydroxide ions combine with any hydrogen ions from acids in the soil to form water. In this way they remove any acidity. The calcium ions attach themselves to the surfaces of fine clay particles in the soil (which have a negative charge). (It is the same sort of effect as rubbing a balloon so that it sticks to your clothes.) Calcium ions have two charges and so can act as links between two clay particles. In this way they bind the soil together, a process called flocculation.

Calcium sulfate

Plaster is made of another important compound of calcium, calcium sulfate.

The material used to make plaster occurs naturally as a soft white rock known as gypsum. It can be made into a fine form and used as a crack filler or poured into molds to make plaster figures. This material is called Plaster of Paris.

Where gypsum is found

Gypsum is found in thick beds, often in the same place as rock salt. This is because gypsum was formed by the evaporation of sea water in ancient seas. It is still being formed in some inland salt lakes, like Australia's Lake Eyre and Utah's Great Salt Lake. Gypsum is cheap to quarry and so is a good material to use in house building, where large amounts of inexpensive materials are needed.

Uses of plaster

Because gypsum is easy to make into a paste and will set hard as it dries, it is used throughout the world as wallboard. The gypsum is put in shallow molds and then covered with a sheet of strong paper. This stops the gypsum board breaking as it is carried about.

Gypsum wallboards are soft and easy to cut into shapes. They also give the very smooth finish that we expect of the walls in our rooms.

▶ Plaster (gypsum and water made into a paste) can be applied with a trowel to finish off a wall. The main wall surfaces are gypsum too, in the form of prefabricated wallboard.

dehydration: the removal of water from a substance.

hydration: the absorption of water by a substance. Hydrated materials are not "wet" but remain firm, apparently dry solids. In some cases hydration makes the substance change color, in many other cases there is no color change, simply a change in volume.

◀ This pictures shows a piece of crystalline gypsum, calcium sulfate. Gypsum is soft enough to be scratched by a nail.

Also...

Plaster of Paris is a special form of the salt calcium sulfate. It is made by heating crushed gypsum to drive off some of the water. It is then crushed to a fine powder. When Plaster of Paris is mixed with water, the calcium sulfate takes up water again (it hydrates) and then sets.

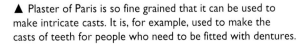

▲ Plaster of Paris is so fine grained that it can be used to make intricate casts. It is, for example, used to make the casts of teeth for people who need to be fitted with dentures.

Bones

Bones are a special form of tissue made by the body cells. Bones are not dead material but living organs. This is why bones will grow together when broken and why they can make new blood for the body.

A bone contains a mixture of living cells and hard mineral that has been deposited by the cells. The mineral is mainly a compound of calcium (in the form of calcium phosphate).

Bone tissue is always renewing itself, shedding old cells and building new ones. To build new cells, bones store the calcium compounds that reach the body through the blood system.

Calcium and growth

When people are young, they grow fast, and therefore the bone cells need large amounts of calcium so that they can make new bone. This is why it is so vital that the food we eat when young contains large amounts of calcium. In later life the body is simply renewing bone, so it needs less calcium.

▲ Because it would not be good for skulls to be made of thick, heavy bone, the calcite of a skull bone is relatively thin. In the case of this beaver skull the ball shape gives strength.

The outer wall of a bone contains plates of calcite. Inside are rods of calcite that carry blood vessels. This is a much softer material, often referred to as bone marrow.

◄▲ Leg and spinal bones are thick because they carry the weight of the body. Nevertheless they are all hollow. This hollow shape, which is similar to a cylinder, is extremely strong. If the bone were solid (like a rod), it would be more easily deformed. A cylinder is also much lighter than a rod.

Teeth

Teeth are a very hard form of calcium carbonate (calcite) specially designed to resist wear. The outer layer of a tooth, called the enamel, has cells arranged in long rods, making them extremely hard and strong.

However, this type of cell is not replaceable in the same way as bones inside the body, which is why teeth do not have the self-repairing properties of other bones and thus must be repaired by dentists.

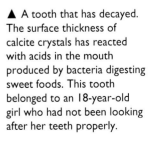

▲ A tooth that has decayed. The surface thickness of calcite crystals has reacted with acids in the mouth produced by bacteria digesting sweet foods. This tooth belonged to an 18-year-old girl who had not been looking after her teeth properly.

Magnesium

Magnesium, like calcium, is a highly reactive element, readily combining with other elements to make compounds.

Magnesium is a silvery metal, not unlike calcium but easier to extract from its ore. It is the most reactive of the metals that can be used in everyday applications (calcium, sodium and potassium are too difficult to produce and are unstable in air, water or both).

The reactivity of magnesium can easily be demonstrated by lighting a taper made of magnesium ribbon. It rapidly bursts into flame giving out a bright white light. (This used to be used for flashlight bulbs; it is still used in signal flares.) Similarly, magnesium reacts quickly with dilute hydrochloric acid, giving off hydrogen gas.

▲▶ Magnesium ribbon. Magnesium reacts with the oxygen of the air and develops a dull oxide coating. The end of this sample has been cleaned with emery paper to show the nature of untarnished metal. The white fragments are of magnesium oxide, formed as the result of burning part of the ribbon (as shown right). The rapid oxidation of the ribbon as it burns is shown by the small pieces of ribbon that are still bright and shiny where the tongs were holding it in the flame.

▲▶ When magnesium ribbon is dropped into dilute hydrochloric acid, a reaction takes place in which hydrogen gas is given off along with a lot of heat.

▲ The most widespread natural use of magnesium is in the chlorophyll in leaves. An ion of magnesium lies at the center of each chlorophyll molecule.

EQUATION: The reaction of magnesium with an acid

Magnesium + dilute hydrochloric acid ➪ *magnesium chloride + hydrogen gas*

$$Mg(s) \quad + \quad 2HCl(aq) \quad ➪ \quad MgCl_2(aq) \quad + \quad H_2(g)$$

Protecting with magnesium

Many metals are subject to corrosion when placed in damp air or damp soil. The most vulnerable of all are iron and steel structures. Small structures can be protected by covering them in a protective coating of, say, paint. However, some iron and steel structures are too big for such treatment. Instead, they are coupled to blocks of metals such as magnesium.

By connecting the metals together in a moist environment, a natural battery is formed. In such a battery, one of the electrodes (the anode) always corrodes, while the other (the cathode) remains undamaged.

The list below shows how magnesium can be used to protect steel. The metals shown in the list (called a reactivity series) will always protect any metal that comes below in the series. Those below act as cathodes, those above act as anodes. Thus magnesium will protect exposed iron because it is more reactive, but tin will not.

REACTIVITY SERIES	
Element	Reactivity
potassium	most reactive
sodium	
calcium	
magnesium	
aluminum	
manganese	
chromium	
zinc	
iron	
cadmium	
tin	
lead	
copper	
mercury	
silver	
gold	
platinum	least reactive

Also...

You may be familiar with the protective role of tin as a plating over steel. Here the tin is used as a kind of paint. However, if the tin plating becomes scratched, you will find the iron corrodes rapidly. This is one reason tin plating is used less today than in the past.

Magnesium oxide

Just as calcium carbonate (limestone) can be heated to produce calcium oxide (quicklime), so magnesium carbonate (dolomite rock) can be heated to release magnesium oxide.

Magnesium oxide, the most useful compound of magnesium, melts at a very high temperature (2800°C). It is a good conductor of heat, but it conducts electricity poorly. These properties allow it to be used to insulate electric heating elements.

anode: the positive electrode of an electrolysis cell.

cathode: the negative electrode of an electrolysis cell.

corrosion: the *slow* decay of a substance resulting from contact with gases and liquids in the environment. The term is often applied to metals. Rust is the corrosion of iron.

electrode: a conductor that forms one terminal of a cell.

◀▼ The reactivity of magnesium relative to iron is demonstrated here. The liquids in both bottles contain an indicator that turns purple when a reaction takes place. The left-hand bottle contains an iron nail with magnesium wrapped around it and the right-hand bottle contains a similar iron nail with tin wrapped around it.

In the left-hand bottle a reaction takes place at the magnesium strip, causing the formation of magnesium hydroxide, an alkaline substance that makes the indicator turn purple. The iron nail is not corroded because magnesium is more reactive than iron.

By contrast, in the right-hand bottle the tin has not reacted and the iron nail has corroded (rusted). This is because iron is more reactive than tin.

◀▼ When a piece of magnesium ribbon is placed in a dish and some copper sulfate solution is added, the magnesium corrodes very rapidly indeed. This is because magnesium is more reactive than copper. Magnesium is also more reactive than iron and can be used to protect it.

▼ Oil storage tanks, and other large steel structures, are often protected from corrosion by attaching them to magnesium blocks buried in the ground. The magnesium blocks corrode, while the steel is protected.

Hard water

There are many compounds dissolved in water. Just as invisible bugs in water can cause great health problems, so invisible chemicals can cause a range of problems for people.

Calcium and magnesium compounds are commonly found in water supplies. If water supplies contain more than 120 mg of calcium and magnesium compounds in each liter of water, the water is described as hard water.

Do you live in a hard-water area?

Most people have a rule of thumb for telling if they live in a hard-water area: if they have trouble getting soapy when in the bath or the shower, then they know they are in a hard-water area.

Most people who live in limestone areas have hard-water supplies, but because water is often transferred for hundreds of kilometers, to match supply and demand, areas far from limestone rocks can also have hard water.

▲ You know you are in a hard-water area if scale forms on a boiler or kettle element quickly and looks like this.

Limescale

Calcium and magnesium carbonates are together usually referred to as limescale. You can sometimes see the thin form of these carbonates build up (precipitate) in many places where hot water is used, such as around the hot water tap in a bathroom, where it gives white smears that thicken to give a dull film.

Carbonates also precipitate quickly on the heating element or side of a coffee jug or electric kettle, because bicarbonates are not stable in hot water.

Also...

Hard water can be either temporary or permanent. Water containing soluble calcium hydrogen carbonate (calcium bicarbonate) is *temporarily hard* because calcium hydrogen carbonates can be removed by boiling (carbonate precipitates). Water is *permanently hard* if it contains calcium or magnesium salts other than the calcium hydrogen carbonates, as these cannot be removed by boiling. It does not produce scale in kettles but it does make it difficult to obtain a lather with soap.

Removing the scale

A wide range of chemicals has been developed to remove limescale from the kitchen, bathroom, hot water system and boiling elements. They have to remove the lime while being safe on the hands. This means that most mineral acids cannot be used. However, natural organic acids can be used to dissolve the scale. Traditionally acetic acid (vinegar) was used, although modern descaling powders contain citric acid (the same acid as in citrus fruit).

Dangers of scaling

As the carbonate layer thickens, it acts like an artificial stone covering, a sort of cultured stalagmite (see page 14). But a cover of stone cannot conduct heat effectively and so the heating element becomes less efficient. As heat cannot get away from the element, there is also a risk that the element will overheat and burn out.

insoluble: a substance that will not dissolve.

precipitate: tiny solid particles formed as a result of a chemical reaction between two liquids or gases. Limescale is a precipitate from hard water.

▲ You know you are in a hard-water area if soap gives little lather.

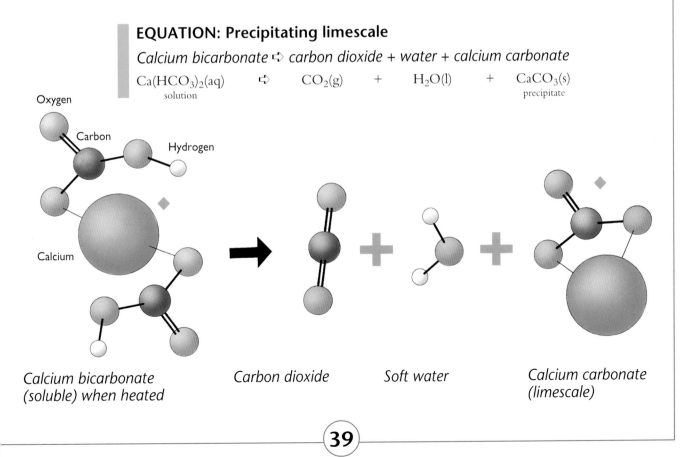

EQUATION: Precipitating limescale

Calcium bicarbonate ⇨ *carbon dioxide + water + calcium carbonate*

$$Ca(HCO_3)_2(aq) \quad ⇨ \quad CO_2(g) \quad + \quad H_2O(l) \quad + \quad CaCO_3(s)$$

solution   precipitate

Oxygen

Carbon

Hydrogen

Calcium

Calcium bicarbonate (soluble) when heated

Carbon dioxide

Soft water

Calcium carbonate (limescale)

Softening water

Hard water – water containing a large amount of dissolved calcium and magnesium salts – can be difficult to use for washing. It makes the wash water develop a soapy scum that is hard to remove. This means that it is very difficult to get cutlery and crockery "squeaky clean," making everything less pleasant to look at.

The same fatty scum also builds up out of sight in the drain pipes and can cause blockages that will need expensive maintenance. Hard water also causes hot water systems to scale up and need frequent repair.

Problems of removing hard water with detergents

A more common method of softening water is to put special chemicals in the wash powder or liquid, so that water is treated as it is used.

A very efficient chemical for this is based on the element phosphorus. This is an element that all plants need for growth. In fact, it is applied to field and gardens as "superphosphate," a kind of fertilizer.

Although the phosphate is good for adding to soils, when used in washing powders phosphate compounds go through sewage plants unaltered and enter rivers. As a result, the water organisms such as algae get huge doses of fertilizer, causing them to grow rapidly (a feature known as algal blooms). Later, when the algae die, the bacteria that decompose their remains take most of the oxygen from the water, causing yet more problems. Because of this, phosphate compounds are no longer used to treat hard water. This is why many detergents advertise "phosphate-free" on their packages.

❶ The granules in the water-softener (either clay or a resin) are charged from common salt. The salt breaks down in water, producing sodium ions that stick to a special artificial honeycomb filter.

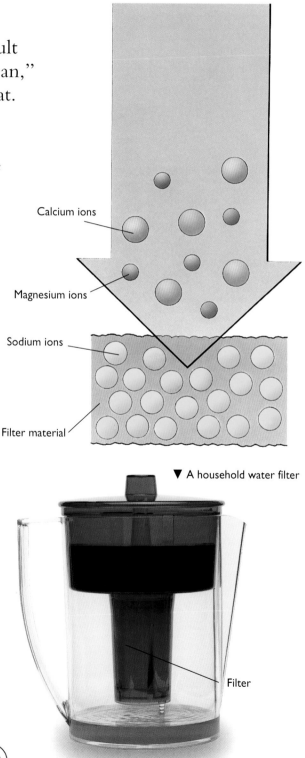

Calcium ions

Magnesium ions

Sodium ions

Filter material

▼ A household water filter

Filter

How water-softeners work

Although most people are prepared to put up with hard-water problems, it is possible to use a chemical means to soften the water. Water-softening is a method of taking away the substances that cause the water to be hard.

One commonly used method is to pass the water entering the house through a tank containing a filter. Modern filters use a special clay mineral or an artificial resin.

The filter absorbs onto its surface material such as common salt, which will react with the calcium and magnesium compounds.

❷ The hard water washes over the filter and the sodium and calcium ions exchange until they are in balance. This takes some of the calcium and magnesium ions out of the water, making it less hard.

ion: an atom, or group of atoms, that has gained or lost one or more electrons and so developed an electrical charge.

resin: resins are natural or synthetic polymers. They can be molded into solid objects or spun into thread.

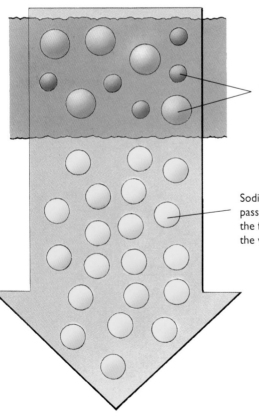

Magnesium and calcium ions left in filter.

Sodium ions pass out of the filter into the water.

▲ This water-softener passes the incoming hard water over artificial resin spheres.

❸ From time to time the filter is recharged by flushing it with salt. This exchanges calcium and magnesium ions for sodium ions.

EQUATION: Water-softening
Hard water (water containing calcium and magnesium compounds in solution)... exchanges for the sodium in salt... leaving calcium and magnesium behind.

Also...

A compound may be bonded together by strong electrical forces. When such a compound dissolves, it splits up, with each of the parts retaining its own electrical charge.

These charged particles are called ions. Calcium ions and magnesium ions have a positive charge, bicarbonate ions have a negative charge. When they re-form into a compound, it will be a neutral substance called a salt.

Water-softening treatments rely on the way that ions can be swapped in and out of a solution.

Antacids

The body makes strong acids to help to digest food. Most of these acids are produced in the lining of the stomach.

The acids are vital and usually the food neutralizes the acids exactly, so that no discomfort is produced. But under some circumstances, especially if we eat a large amount of food and do not chew it properly, the digestive system does not balance.

Neutralizing

One way to counteract the occasional problem of indigestion is to use a substance, such as calcium carbonate, that reacts with an acid. "Antacids" are normally taken in powder form, as a tablet, or sometimes as a suspension in water. Calcium bicarbonate is also used because it is soluble and can be mixed more easily with water.

Magnesium hydroxide can be mixed in water and made into a suspension. The result is called "Milk of Magnesia." Because it is only a suspension, over time the magnesium hydroxide settles to the bottom of the bottle. This is why it is important to shake the bottle before use.

Magnesium hydroxide has an advantage over calcium carbonate. When it reacts with acids, it does not produce carbon dioxide, so there is no embarrassing burping after taking milk of magnesia, as there might be after taking calcium bicarbonate!

▲ Magnesium hydroxide, Milk of Magnesia, is a traditional antacid. Notice that it is a mixture (a suspension of magnesium hydroxide in water). Over time the suspension settles out. The precipitate shows clearly at the bottom of this bottle.

EQUATION: Neutralizing stomach acid with a hydroxide

Hydrochloric acid + magnesium hydroxide ⇨ magnesium chloride + water

$$2HCl(aq) \quad + \quad Mg(OH)_2(aq) \quad ⇨ \quad MgCl_2(aq) \quad + \quad 2H_2O(l)$$

Chlorine

Magnesium

Hydrogen

Oxygen

The gas that tells of success

The action of a carbonate antacid is to produce a gas. When this builds up in the digestive system, it is released quite uncontrollably as a "burp."

However, the gas that occurs in some fizzing antacid tablets is formed in the glass. This is because the manufacturers put citric acid powder in with the calcium carbonate. When the tablet is put in water, the acid and carbonate react to release carbon dioxide and give an attractive impression of action even before the antacid is digested.

acid: compounds containing hydrogen that can attack and dissolve many substances.

neutralization: the reaction of acids and bases to produce a salt and water. The reaction causes hydrogen from the acid and hydroxide from the base to be changed to water. For example, hydrochloric acid reacts with sodium hydroxide to form common salt and water. The term is more generally used for any reaction in which the pH changes toward 7.0, which is the pH of a neutral solution.

Carbon dioxide gas in belch

◀▶ Indigestion tablets may contain calcium or magnesium carbonate or bicarbonate. Here you can see some tablets reacting vigorously with dilute hydrochloric acid just as takes place in your stomach. The bubbles are carbon dioxide gas.

Why too much acid is produced

The digestive system is triggered into releasing acids to match the volume of food we eat. So if we eat a lot, a great deal of acid is released from the linings of the digestive system.

Acids work on the surfaces of food, so the better it is chewed, the faster the acids can get to work. If food is eaten in large lumps (i.e., it is bolted down), the acid will not be able to get to it quickly. As a result the amount of acid produced can be more than is needed for digestion. The excess acid then starts to attack the linings of the digestive system, causing the pains that are known as indigestion and heartburn. Bacteria working in this very acid environment can even cause ulcers.

Acid released from stomach lining

Calcium carbonate reacts with acids

Digestive juices in stomach broken down by acids

EQUATION: Neutralizing stomach acid with a carbonate

Hydrochloric acid + calcium carbonate ➪ calcium chloride + water + carbon dioxide gas

$$2HCl(aq) \quad + \quad CaCO_3(s) \quad ➪ \quad CaCl_2(aq) \quad + \quad 2H_2O(l) \quad + \quad CO_2(g)$$

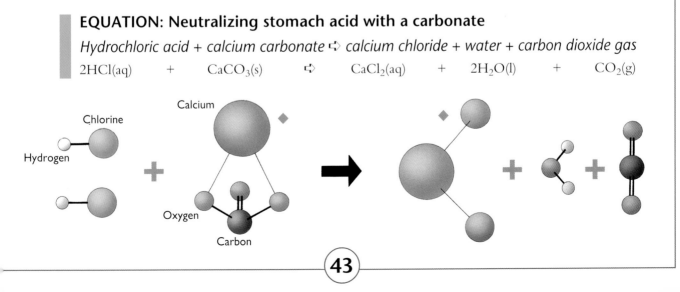

Chlorine

Calcium

Hydrogen

Oxygen

Carbon

The Periodic Table

Actinium (Ac)	89	Calcium (Ca)	20	Fermium (Fm)	100		
Aluminum (Al)	13	Californium (Cf)	98	Fluorine (F)	9		
Antimony (Sb)	51	Carbon (C)	6	Francium (Fr)	87		
Americium (Am)	95	Cerium (Ce)	58	Gadolinium (Gd)	64		
Argon (Ar)	18	Cesium (Cs)	55	Gallium (Ga)	31		
Arsenic (As)	33	Chlorine (Cl)	17	Germanium (Ge)	32		
Astatine (At)	85	Chromium (Cr)	24	Gold (Au)	79		
Barium (Ba)	56	Cobalt (Co)	27	Hafnium (Hf)	72		
Berkelium (Bk)	97	Copper (Cu)	29	Hassium (Hs)	108		
Beryllium (Be)	4	Curium (Cm)	96	Helium (He)	2		
Bismuth (Bi)	83	Dubnium (Db)	105	Holmium (Ho)	67		
Bohrium (Bh)	107	Dysprosium (Dy)	66	Hydrogen (H)	1		
Boron (B)	5	Einsteinium (Es)	99	Indium (In)	49		
Bromine (Br)	35	Erbium (Er)	68	Iodine (I)	53		
Cadmium (Cd)	48	Europium (Eu)	63	Iridium (Ir)	77		

GROUPS ▶

PERIODS ▼

Transition metals

	1 (1)	2 (2)	(3)	(4)	(5)	(6)	(7)	(8
1	1 **H** Hydrogen 1							
2	3 **Li** Lithium 7	4 **Be** Beryllium 9						
3	11 **Na** Sodium 23	12 **Mg** Magnesium 24						
4	19 **K** Potassium 39	20 **Ca** Calcium 40	21 **Sc** Scandium 45	22 **Ti** Titanium 48	23 **V** Vanadium 51	24 **Cr** Chromium 52	25 **Mn** Manganese 55	26 **F** Iron 56
5	37 **Rb** Rubidium 85	38 **Sr** Strontium 88	39 **Y** Yttrium 89	40 **Zr** Zirconium 91	41 **Nb** Niobium 93	42 **Mo** Molybdenum 96	43 **Tc** Technetium (99)	44 **R** Ruthe 10
6	55 **Cs** Cesium 133	56 **Ba** Barium 137	71 **Lu** Lutetium 175	72 **Hf** Hafnium 178	73 **Ta** Tantalum 181	74 **W** Tungsten 184	75 **Re** Rhenium 186	76 **O** Osmi 19
7	87 **Fr** Francium (223)	88 **Ra** Radium (226)	103 **Lr** Lawrencium (260)	104 **Rf** Rutherfordium (261)	105 **Db** Dubnium (262)	106 **Sg** Seaborgium (263)	107 **Bh** Bohrium (262)	10 **H** Hassi (26

Legend:
- Metals
- Metalloids (semimetals)
- Nonmetals
- Inner transition metals

Lanthanide series

57 **La** Lanthanum 139	58 **Ce** Cerium 140	59 **Pr** Praseodymium 141	60 **N** Neodyr 14

Actinide series

89 **Ac** Actinium (227)	90 **Th** Thorium (232)	91 **Pa** Protactinium (231)	92 **U** Uran (23

Iron (Fe)	26	Neptunium (Np)	93	Protactinium (Pa)	91	Strontium (Sr)	38	Ununoctium (Uuo)	118
Krypton (Kr)	36	Nickel (Ni)	28	Radium (Ra)	88	Sulfur (S)	16	Ununquadium (Uuq)	114
Lanthanum (La)	57	Niobium (Nb)	41	Radon (Rn)	86	Tantalum (Ta)	73	Unununium (Uuu)	111
Lawrencium (Lr)	103	Nitrogen (N)	7	Rhenium (Re)	75	Technetium (Tc)	43	Uranium (U)	92
Lead (Pb)	82	Nobelium (No)	102	Rhodium (Rh)	45	Tellurium (Te)	52	Vanadium (V)	23
Lithium (Li)	3	Osmium (Os)	76	Rubidium (Rb)	37	Terbium (Tb)	65	Xenon (Xe)	54
Lutetium (Lu)	71	Oxygen (O)	8	Ruthenium (Ru)	44	Thallium (Tl)	81	Ytterbium (Yb)	70
Magnesium (Mg)	12	Palladium (Pd)	46	Rutherfordium (Rf)	104	Thorium (Th)	90	Yttrium (Y)	39
Manganese (Mn)	25	Phosphorus (P)	15	Samarium (Sm)	62	Thulium (Tm)	69	Zinc (Zn)	30
Meitnerium (Mt)	109	Platinum (Pt)	78	Scandium (Sc)	21	Tin (Sn)	50	Zirconium (Zr)	40
Mendelevium (Md)	101	Plutonium (Pu)	94	Seaborgium (Sg)	106	Titanium (Ti)	22		
Mercury (Hg)	80	Polonium (Po)	84	Selenium (Se)	34	Tungsten (W)	74		
Molybdenum (Mo)	42	Potassium (K)	19	Silicon (Si)	14	Ununbium (Uub)	112		
Neodymium (Nd)	60	Praseodymium (Pr)	59	Silver (Ag)	47	Ununhexium (Uuh)	116		
Neon (Ne)	10	Promethium (Pm)	61	Sodium (Na)	11	Ununnilium (Uun)	110		

				3	4	5	6	7	8 or 0
9)	(10)	(11)	(12)	(13)	(14)	(15)	(16)	(17)	(18)
									2 **He** Helium 4
				5 **B** Boron 11	6 **C** Carbon 12	7 **N** Nitrogen 14	8 **O** Oxygen 16	9 **F** Fluorine 19	10 **Ne** Neon 20
				13 **Al** Aluminum 27	14 **Si** Silicon 28	15 **P** Phosphorus 31	16 **S** Sulfur 32	17 **Cl** Chlorine 35	18 **Ar** Argon 40
27 **Co** Cobalt 59	28 **Ni** Nickel 59	29 **Cu** Copper 64	30 **Zn** Zinc 65	31 **Ga** Gallium 70	32 **Ge** Germanium 73	33 **As** Arsenic 75	34 **Se** Selenium 79	35 **Br** Bromine 80	36 **Kr** Krypton 84
45 **Rh** Rhodium 103	46 **Pd** Palladium 106	47 **Ag** Silver 108	48 **Cd** Cadmium 112	49 **In** Indium 115	50 **Sn** Tin 119	51 **Sb** Antimony 122	52 **Te** Tellurium 128	53 **I** Iodine 127	54 **Xe** Xenon 131
77 **Ir** Iridium 192	78 **Pt** Platinum 195	79 **Au** Gold 197	80 **Hg** Mercury 201	81 **Tl** Thallium 204	82 **Pb** Lead 207	83 **Bi** Bismuth 209	84 **Po** Polonium (209)	85 **At** Astatine (210)	86 **Rn** Radon (222)
109 **Mt** Meitnerium (266)	110 **Uun** Ununnilium (272)	111 **Uuu** Unununium (272)	112 **Uub** Ununbium (277)		114 **Uuq** Ununquadium (289)		116 **Uuh** Ununhexium (289)		118 **Uuo** Ununoctium (293)

61 **Pm** Promethium (145)	62 **Sm** Samarium 150	63 **Eu** Europium 152	64 **Gd** Gadolinium 157	65 **Tb** Terbium 159	66 **Dy** Dysprosium 163	67 **Ho** Holmium 165	68 **Er** Erbium 167	69 **Tm** Thulium 169	70 **Yb** Ytterbium 173
93 **Np** Neptunium (237)	94 **Pu** Plutonium (244)	95 **Am** Americium (243)	96 **Cm** Curium (247)	97 **Bk** Berkelium (247)	98 **Cf** Californium (251)	99 **Es** Einsteinium (252)	100 **Fm** Fermium (257)	101 **Md** Mendelevium (258)	102 **No** Nobelium (259)

Understanding equations

As you read through Volumes 1 to 15 in the Elements set, you will notice that many pages contain equations using symbols. Symbols make it easy for chemists to write out the reactions that are occurring in a way that allows a better understanding of the processes involved. If you are not familiar with these symbols, these pages explain them.

Symbols for the elements

The basis for the modern use of symbols for elements dates back to the 19th century. At that time a shorthand was developed using the first letter of the element wherever possible.

Thus O stands for oxygen, H stands for hydrogen, and so on. However, if we were to use only the first letter, there could be some confusion. For example, nitrogen and nickel would both use the symbols N. To overcome this problem, many element symbols take the first two letters of the full name, with the second letter in lowercase. So, although nitrogen is N, nickel becomes Ni. Not all symbols come from the English name; many use the Latin name instead. That is why, for example, gold is not G but Au (from the Latin *aurum*), and sodium has the symbol Na (from the Latin *natrium*).

Compounds of elements are made by combining letters. So, the molecule carbon

Written and symbolic equations

In this book important chemical equations are briefly stated in words (they are called word equations) and are then shown in their symbolic form along with the states.

What reaction the equation illustrates

EQUATION: The formation of calcium hydroxide

Word equation —————— Calcium oxide + water ⇨ calcium hydroxide

Symbol equation ————— $CaO(s)$ + $H_2O(l)$ ⇨ $Ca(OH)_2(aq)$

heated

Sometimes you will find additional descriptions below the symbolic equation.

Symbol showing the state: *s* is for solid, *l* is for liquid, *g* is for gas, and *aq* is for aqueous.

Diagrams

Some of the equations are shown as graphic representations.

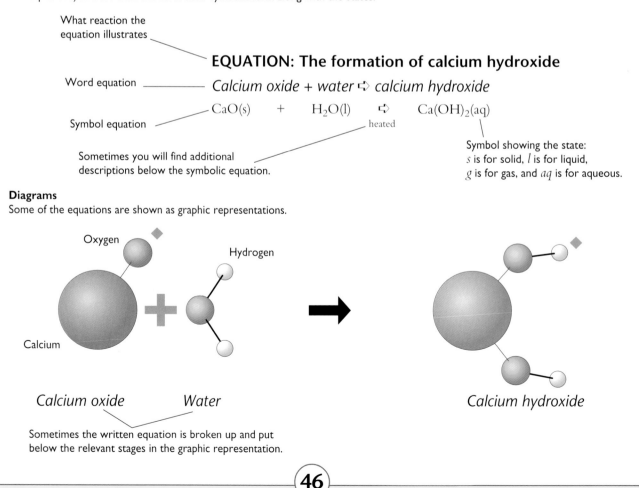

Oxygen

Hydrogen

Calcium

Calcium oxide   Water

Calcium hydroxide

Sometimes the written equation is broken up and put below the relevant stages in the graphic representation.

monoxide is CO. By using lowercase letters for the second letter of an element, it is possible to show that cobalt, symbol Co, is not the same as the molecule carbon monoxide, CO.

However, the letters can be made to do much more than this. In many molecules atoms combine in unequal numbers. So, for example, carbon dioxide has one atom of carbon for every two of oxygen. That is shown by using the number 2 beside the oxygen, and the symbol becomes CO_2.

In practice some groups of atoms combine as a unit with other substances. Thus, for example, calcium bicarbonate (one of the compounds used in some antacid pills) is written $Ca(HCO_3)_2$. This shows that the part of the substance inside the parentheses reacts as a unit, and the 2 outside the parentheses shows the presence of two such units.

Some substances attract water molecules to themselves. To show this, a dot is used. So, the blue form of copper sulfate is written $CuSO_4.5H_2O$. In this case five molecules of water attract to one of copper sulfate. When you see the dot, you know that this water can be driven off by heating; it is part of the crystal structure.

In a reaction substances change by rearranging the combinations of atoms. The way they change is shown by using the chemical symbols, placing those that will react (the starting materials, or reactants) on the left and the products of the reaction on the right. Between the two an arrow shows which way the reaction is going.

It is possible to describe a reaction in words. That produces word equations, which are given throughout Volumes 1 to 15. However, it is easier to understand what is happening by using an equation containing symbols. They are also given in many places. They are not shown when the equations are very complex.

In any equation both sides balance; that is, there must be an equal number of like atoms on both sides of the arrow. When you try to write down reactions, you, too, must balance your equation; you cannot have a few atoms left over at the end!

The symbols in parentheses are abbreviations for the physical state of each substance taking part, so that (s) is used for solid, (l) for liquid, (g) for gas, and (aq) for an aqueous solution, that is, a solution of a substance dissolved in water.

Atoms and ions
Each sphere represents a particle of an element. A particle can be an atom or an ion. Each atom or ion is associated with other atoms or ions through bonds – forces of attraction. The size of the particles and the nature of the bonds can be extremely important in determining the nature of the reaction or the properties of the compound.

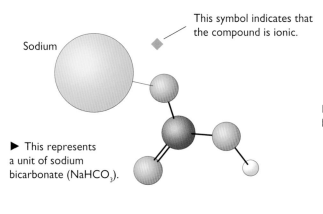

Sodium

This symbol indicates that the compound is ionic.

▶ This represents a unit of sodium bicarbonate ($NaHCO_3$).

The term "unit" is sometimes used to simplify the representation of a combination of ions.

Chemical symbols, equations, and diagrams
The arrangement of any molecule or compound can be shown in one of the two ways shown below, depending on which gives the clearer picture. The left-hand image is called a ball-and-stick diagram because it uses rods and spheres to show the structure of the material. This example shows water, H_2O. There are two hydrogen atoms and one oxygen atom.

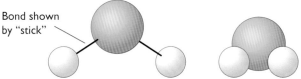

Bond shown by "stick"

Colors too
The colors of each of the particles help differentiate the elements involved. The diagram can then be matched to the written and symbolic equation given with the diagram. In the case above, oxygen is red, and hydrogen is gray.

Key facts about...

Name: calcium
Symbol: Ca
Atomic number: 20
Atomic weight: 40.07
Position in Periodic Table: group 2 (2)
(alkaline earth metal); period 4
State at room temperature: solid
Color: silvery
Density of solid: 1.55 g/cc
Melting point: 842°C
Boiling point: 1,494°C
Origin of name: from the Latin word
calx, meaning lime
Shell pattern of electrons: 2–8–8–2
*Further facts on this element can be found in
Volume 16: Actinium to Fluorine*

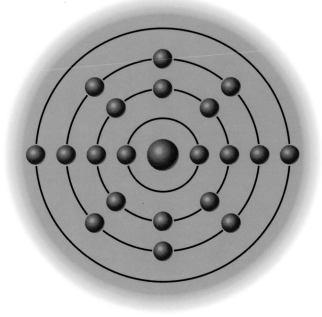

Name: magnesium
Symbol: Mg
Atomic number: 12
Atomic weight: 24.31
Position in Periodic Table: group 2 (2)
(alkaline earth metal); period 3
State at room temperature: solid
Color: silvery-white
Density of solid: 1.74 g/cc
Melting point: 650°C
Boiling point: 1,107°C
Origin of name: from the Greek word
Magnesia, a district of Greece.
Shell pattern of electrons: 2–8–2
*Further facts on this element can be found in
Volume 17: Francium to Polonium*

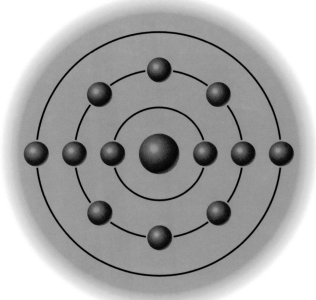

Glossary of technical terms

acid: compounds containing hydrogen that can attack and dissolve many substances. Acids are described as weak or strong, dilute or concentrated, mineral or organic.

acidity: a general term for the strength of an acid in a solution.

anion: a negatively charged atom or group of atoms.

anode: the negative terminal of a battery or the positive electrode of an electrolysis cell.

base: a compound that may be soapy to the touch and that can react with an acid in water to form a salt and water.

calcite: the crystalline form of calcium carbonate.

cathode: the positive terminal of a battery or the negative electrode of an electrolysis cell.

cation: a positively charged atom or group of atoms.

caustic: a substance that can cause burns if it touches the skin.

compound: a chemical consisting of two or more elements chemically bonded together. Calcium atoms can combine with carbon atoms and oxygen atoms to make calcium carbonate, a compound of all three atoms.

coral reef: a region of the seabed where corals grow in massive banks.

corrosion: the *slow* decay of a substance resulting from contact with gases and liquids in the environment. The term is often applied to metals. Rust is the corrosion of iron.

decompose: to break down a substance (for example, by heat or with the aid of a catalyst) into simpler components. In such a chemical reaction only one substance is involved.

dehydration: the removal of water from a substance by heating it, placing it in a dry atmosphere or using a drying agent.

dilute acid: an acid whose concentration has been reduced by a large proportion of water.

dissolve: to break down a substance in a solution without reacting.

electrode: a conductor that forms one terminal of a cell.

facing: sheets of stone cut to form the decorative outer surface of a building. It is a form of cladding. On modern buildings it is also sometimes called siding.

kiln: a structure designed for baking minerals. Lime, brick and pottery kilns are all common.

hydration: the absorption of water by a substance. Hydrated materials are not "wet" but remain firm, apparently dry solids. In some cases hydration makes the substance change color, in many other cases there is no color change, simply a change in volume.

insoluble: a substance that will not dissolve.

ion: an atom that has gained or lost an electron and so developed an electrical charge. Ions behave differently from electrically neutral atoms and molecules. They can move in an electric field and they can also bind strongly to solvent molecules such as water. Positively charged ions are called cations; negatively charged ions are called anions. Ions carry electrical current through solutions.

lava: a name for molten rock that pours from volcanoes. The word is also used for the solid rock that forms from the liquid.

mineral: a solid substance made of just one element or chemical compound. Calcite is a mineral because it consists only of calcium carbonate; halite is a mineral because it contains only sodium chloride; quartz is a mineral because it consists of only silicon dioxide.

mineral-laden: a solution close to saturation.

neutralization: the reaction of acids and bases to produce a salt and water. The reaction causes hydrogen from the acid and hydroxide from the base to be changed to water. For example, hydrochloric acid reacts with sodium hydroxide to form common salt and water. The term is more generally used for any reaction in which the pH changes toward 7.0, which is the pH of a neutral solution.

ore: a rock containing enough of a useful substance to make mining it worthwhile.

oxidation: a reaction in which the oxidizing agent removes electrons. (Note that oxidizing agents do not have to contain oxygen.)

percolate: to move slowly through the pores of a rock.

porous: a material containing many small holes or cracks. Quite often the pores are connected, and liquids, such as water or oil, can move through them.

precipitate: tiny solid particles formed as a result of a chemical reaction between two liquids or gases.

prospector: a person who is exploring for geologically rich deposits of metals and gemstones.

reaction: the recombination of two substances using parts of each substance to produce new substances.

resin: resins are natural or synthetic polymers. They can be molded into solid objects or spun into thread.

saturated: a state in which a liquid can hold no more of a substance. If any more of the substance is added, it will not dissolve.

solution: a mixture of a liquid and at least one other substance (e.g., saltwater). Mixtures can be separated by physical means, for example, by evaporation and cooling.

stable: able to exist without changing into another substance.

weather: a term used by Earth scientists and derived from "weathering." It means to react with water and gases of the environment.

weathering: the slow natural processes that break down rocks and reduce them to small fragments either by mechanical or chemical means.

Set Index

A